MARY
REMEMBERS

MARY REMEMBERS: AN ADVENT BIBLE STUDY

By

Richard E. Davies

Macon, GA

An Ina and Elsie Memorial Publication

Dedicated to two United Methodist Congregations:
Rico, Georgia and
Martha Bowman Memorial in Macon, Georgia.
Thanks to both of them for allowing
me to lead trial versions of this study.

TABLE OF CONTENTS

Writing on Wax

On page 8 are two scenes showing how notes were taken and rough drafts written in ancient times. Writing was done on wax tablets, which were inexpensive and could easily be corrected. Whenever the recorded information was no longer needed, the wax could be smoothed for re-use. The writing was transcribed in pen and ink after it was perfected.

As the Gospel writer, Luke, pursued his historical research, he would have taken extensive notes on such wax tablets.

In the pictures on page 8 we see the goddess, Athena, recording a man's athletic victories, shown on a vase displayed in the Antikensammlung, Munich, Germany, and a mosaic of Clio, the muse of history, displayed in the Roman National Museum-Palazzo Massimo.

INTRODUCTION

The mother of Jesus should be an inspiration to all. Consider the real difficulties of raising a precocious child. Then consider the additional difficulties of raising the Son of God. Mary must have been special. She was not chosen at random.

I hope a person who reads this book will be reading it with a companion or study partner, or, better yet, with a small group of like-minded people. I hope this book will lead to meaningful religious reflection as well as reflection on the reader's own life.

This book is written from the perspective of Protestant Christianity, a perspective that has sometimes discounted the importance of the life of the Blessed Virgin Mary. Instead, Mary has sometimes been used as a token in theological battles between Protestant factions. The issue has been her virginity, not her life. In these battles, one side affirms her virginity and the other side rejects it, and neither side takes any consideration of the mother of Jesus, her humanity, and her influence on her Son and his work.

In this brief study we will look at what we know and what we can plausibly infer about Mary (as a real person) based on the New Testament and our knowledge of the times in which she lived. We will also take seriously one specific tradition about her life, the tradition that she spent the final years of her life in the city of Ephesus.

We know that John, son of Zebedee, and one of Jesus' closest disciples, spent his last years in Ephesus, and when Jesus was on the cross he gave John responsibility for the care of Mary. I think that when Luke accompanied Paul to Ephesus he had a chance to interview Mary. Luke was not one of the 12; he never knew Jesus in the flesh. Luke was a historian, and I think much that we read in Luke's *Gospel* was told to him by Mary.

As a historian, Luke interviewed anyone he could who had known Jesus, and he apparently had a copy of *Mark's Gospel*, so Mary was not his only source, but she was an important source.

Let me say something about special features of this book. I have distinguished between people named Matthew, Mark, Luke and John and books written by these people by putting words in italics whenever I'm referring to something written in the Bible. There are no italics when I am simply referring to people.

This book is intended to guide weekly study during the four weeks of Advent (the four weeks prior to Christmas). Following these four chapters are some additional resources.

Keep in mind that this book is a guide to Bible study. Keep your Bible handy as you read this book. Please read the material in the Bible that we refer to.

May this book be a blessing to you.

✠ Richard Davies

A YOUNG GIRL MAKES A BIG DECISION

Matthew and Luke each give us different information. Matthew tells us that Joseph was betrothed to
Mary. Our customs today are different than they were in
the time of Jesus, but it will help us to think of them being
engaged. *Matthew 1:18-19* tells us that, after betrothal,
Joseph discovered that his bride-to-be was pregnant and he
knew he was not the father. It would be normal for a man
to break the engagement, but he had a dream in which
God's angel told him that he should marry the girl. The
baby was God's own child and Joseph should call the
child "Jesus" (which in Hebrew is the same as "Joshua.")

That's not much information, but *Luke* tells us
more. *Matthew* mentions her only one more time (*13:55*),
and it is an indirect reference. *Luke* becomes our most
important source for understanding Mary.

The angel Gabriel was sent from God
to a young woman named Mary in
Nazareth, a town of Galilee. She was to be
married to man named Joseph of the
family of David. When the angel came to
her he said: "Hail, highly honored one! God
is with you!"
She was startled by his words and
wondered what such a greeting might
mean. But the angel said to her, "Fear not,
Mary, for you have found favor with God.
You will have a son and will name him

15

Jesus. He will be great and will be called the Son of the Most High."

Then Mary said to the angel, "How can this be, for I am not yet married?" The angel answered her, "The Holy Spirit will come upon you and the power of the Most High will cover you; therefore your child will be called holy, the Son of God." Mary said, "I am God's servant. May it be with me as you say." Then the angel left her.

(*Luke 1:26-38,* Sherman and Kent. This version is shortened. Read the full account in your own Bible.)

Many of us have heard this story at Christmas every year of our lives so that nothing in it surprises us. In spite of this, everything in this story should surprise us.

Why Should Mary Have Been Afraid?

First, what is an angel? You probably know that an angel is a messenger from God. What else? Angels are fierce warriors. We tend to forget this aspect of angels because we mostly associate them with the cute children in church Christmas plays. We can remind ourselves about how tough angels are by reading *Numbers 22:22-33.* When you read this passage in *Numbers* you will see that it is a small part of a much larger story, but these verses are enough to remind us about angels.

In *Numbers*, Balaam is a "prophet" who is not like the Prophets of God. The Bible tells us about Prophets of God and includes books by some of these Prophets (*Isaiah, Jeremiah, Ezekiel*, etc.); all of them fearlessly speak God's word in spite of the fact that they may become unpopular (or even killed) when people react against God's standards. In contrast, Balaam was a "prophet for hire." He would say anything his employer wanted him to say, and those who hired him thought that God would be required to do whatever Balaam said. This sounds strange, but Balaam's employers were convinced that Balaam could control God.

That's why God got angry and sent the angel. Balaam was supposed to go to the top of a mountain to speak his prophecy against Israel, and he couldn't see the angel who was blocking his way. Finally Balaam's own donkey, which was wiser than Balaam was, had to explain the situation. After that Balaam could see and hear the angel, and it is at that point in the story that we discover how dangerous angels might be. The angel actually threatened to kill Balaam.

Mary was Strong and Confident.

Now we understand why, when the angel came to Mary, he said, "Don't be afraid."

Was Mary afraid? What do you think? Keep in mind that we are dealing with a memory. We think Luke includes this story because he heard it from Mary, and Luke probably met Mary 50 or more years after Jesus had been born. Mary doesn't seem to remember being afraid. If she had told Luke, "This angel popped up and scared me almost to death," Luke would have written something about her being afraid. Instead, Luke portrays Mary as being curious. She "pondered" (*Luke 1:29*).

After telling Mary not to be afraid, Gabriel launched into a complicated speech about world history and cosmic eternity (*Luke 1:32-33*).

At this moment we discover something about Mary and why God chose her. She kept her wits and asked questions. She said, "I'm not concerned about world history and cosmic eternity. Tell me about today and tomorrow and the next nine months. I'm a virgin, and virgins don't usually have babies." (I think this is what verse 34 means.)

At this point the story is a bit humorous if we can step back to appreciate it. Gabriel was tremendously excited about the Son of God. Also, angels don't live the life that people live, so they don't have a deep personal understanding of people's concerns. There's a difference between being told about something and actually experiencing it, and angels have only been told about human life. So, in his excitement, Gabriel forgot what he had been told about people and expressed his great joy about the Son of God. Gabriel forgot that people are normally born as a result of the intimate relationship between their father and mother. We can imagine Mary using the "time out" sign to get Gabriel to stop talking and allow her a chance to ask her questions.

Never forget that every event described in the Bible is shortened. In the Bible, conversations and speeches are always summarized. Gabriel and Mary had a much longer conversation than what we read.

At the end of the conversation the young girl agreed and the tough soldier-angel left satisfied. He had been less satisfied with his earlier assignment, a conversation with Mary's uncle Zechariah, father of John the Baptist (*Luke 1:12-20*). Zechariah had been terrified and then didn't trust God's own angel.

Mary was a Disciple

At this point, let's realize that the mother of Jesus was also a disciple of Jesus. New Testament scholar Raymond Brown has said that there are specific qualities we find in any disciple:

✠First, a disciple hears the call of God. To understand this, think about the fishermen who became disciples of Jesus. He went to them and said, "Follow me." They heard the call of God.

✛Second, a disciple says, "Yes." Think again about the fishermen. They left their nets and boats and went with Jesus.

✛Third, a disciple tells someone else. Jesus called Andrew, and Andrew told his brother, Peter. Without his brother, Andrew, the Big Fisherman, Peter, would have kept on fishing, and would never have known Jesus.

✛Notice that this understanding of discipleship does not imply that a "disciple" had to be one of a small, select group that traveled with Jesus. Many, many people can be   disciples, including you and me.

The scholar I mentioned, Raymond Brown, says the same qualities apply to Mary:

(1) The angel Gabriel came to her and said something like, "Hello, Mary, God is with you." This seemed to be a strange greeting, but Mary listened. That's the first requirement of a disciple.

(2) When the angel got done with his message, Mary agreed, saying, "I am a servant of the Lord. Let it be as you have said." That's the second requirement.

(3) You remember the first thing Mary did after the angel left. She got up and went to see her cousin, Elizabeth, and told her all about it. That caps it off. Mary was a disciple.

Furthermore, she was not just a disciple for nine months, or even until the baby grew up and was able to take care of himself. She was a disciple for the rest of her life. We need to understand that it is not easy to be a disciple. After Jesus was born, we are told that Mary had to think seriously about the meaning of this baby. (*Luke 2:19, 51.*) Every disciple we find in the New Testament had questions and lapses of faith. In *Mark 3:21*, we read that early in Jesus' ministry the family was afraid that he had gone nuts. They set out to bring him home, and he told people that they were not his real family. Jesus said, "Whoever does the will of God is my brother and sister and mother." (*Mark 3:35, Luke 8:21.*) What sort of statement is that? I think it was a teaching moment for his disciple-mother. We have more thoughts about this in the additional material at the end of this book.

She went along with Jesus, and probably the rest of her family, to the wedding at Cana, where he turned water into wine. (*John 2:1-11*).

Finally, we read about her being at the cross, watching her son die (*John 19:25*), and after the resurrection, she was one of the group of disciples who gathered in the upper room (*Acts 1:14*).

Thus we find that Mary was a disciple. She would continue to be a disciple for the rest of her life. Maybe she had always been a disciple.

Questions for Discussion

If the angel had come to you, what do you think your response would have been? Would you have been able to think, ponder, and ask questions? Would you have been afraid? Would you have been too startled to make any response?

Read *Luke 1:12-20* and spend some time discussing why Zechariah and Mary were so different in their responses.

When Gabriel and Mary discussed the Son of God, what do you imagine they said? Can you imagine their extended conversation that is summarized in *Luke's Gospel*?

Do you think Mary could have been a disciple before Jesus actually came to earth and was born as a human? Why or why not? Could Mary have been a disciple before the angel came to her?

# MARY SANG A GREAT SONG

When Gabriel came to Mary she listened, asked questions for clarification, agreed to become the mother of her Lord, and immediately went to Elizabeth to tell her about the coming Son of God. That's why Brown calls her the first disciple.

Luke shares with us a wonderful song that Mary sang when she visited Elizabeth (*Luke 1:46-55*, KJV altered):

> Mary said, My soul magnifies the Lord,
> And my spirit has rejoiced in God my Savior.
> For he has regarded the low estate of his handmaiden: for, behold, from henceforth all generations shall call me blessed.
> For he that is mighty has done to me great things; and holy is his name.
> And his mercy is on them that fear him from generation to generation.
> He has shown strength with his arm; he has scattered the proud in the imagination of their hearts.
> He has put down the mighty from their seats, and exalted them of low degree.
> He has filled the hungry with good things; and the rich he has sent empty away.
> He has helped his servant Israel, in remembrance of his mercy;
> As he spoke to our fathers, to Abraham, and to his seed for ever.

Can you imagine Luke going up to Mary's house, sitting down with his wax tablet, and asking her, "What did you and Elizabeth talk about when you stayed with her?" Mary told Luke how surprised she was when Elizabeth greeted her (*Luke 1:41-45*). She told Luke, "You know, Zechariah and Elizabeth were just ordinary people. Zechariah was a priest, but that didn't give him any income, and when I knew him he was almost too old to do any work that paid. They didn't have much, but they welcomed me. My family didn't have much either. All of us were just ordinary people. Isn't it wonderful how God uses ordinary people? It's always been like that."

Then Mary said, "Surely you remember Samuel from the old days! His mother, Hannah, was ordinary, just like us, and when he was born God gave her a song (*1 Samuel 2:1-10*). God put that song in my heart and Elizabeth and I talked about it."

Then Mary sang her version of what Hannah had sung. Just like Hannah, she sang about God blessing the poor and hungry and sending the proud and rich away. The conversations that Mary and Elizabeth had must have cemented Mary's understanding of God's plans, and she must have taught these things to Jesus as soon as he was able to understand.

Luke's conversations with Mary must be the reason that he tells us about the important parables on this theme which are not in the other three gospels:

The parable of the rich man and Lazarus (*Luke 16:19-31*) shows us that we have a responsibility to help the poor people we encounter day after day.

The parable about the Pharisee and the tax collector praying in the Temple (*Luke 18:9-14*) shows us that we should not be "self-satisfied," because those who are "proud" will be scattered. Jesus taught the same sort of message when he gave advice about where to sit when you are invited to a dinner (*Luke 14:7-11*).

Mary also sang about a second chance (or third, or fourth, or fifth . . .) when she sang, "God has helped his servant Israel . . ." The Old Testament is about many "second" chances. The Old Testament is a saga about Israel forsaking God, God giving Israel another chance, Israel forsaking God . . . and on and on.

Mary's Son taught about second chances. He told a parable about a man planting a tree that didn't produce fruit, so the man ordered the tree to be cut down. The gardener asked the man to give the tree a second chance: he would fertilize it and tend it carefully. After that, if it didn't produce fruit, the gardener would agree to cutting it down (*Luke 13:6-9*).This is another parable that only Luke tells us about.

Maybe the most important thing in Mary's song is, "He has . . . exalted them of low degree." Jesus didn't just teach us about this. Jesus showed us what it means.

In *Philippians 2:8-9*, we read: "He humbled himself and became obedient to the point of death, even death on a cross. Therefore God highly exalted him." In Jesus' time the authorities crucified many people. Each crucifixion was intended to be an example to everyone else that the government of the Roman Empire was in charge and had the power to humiliate anyone. Crucifixions were carried out next to well-traveled roads so that everyone passing by would know that they must respect the Roman government. If they didn't they might suffer the shame of being crucified. Not only was it serious, painful torture, but nothing was more shameful.

Mary must have grieved when her Son was crucified, but she was not ashamed to stay with him. When Luke interviewed her and she shared the song, she also explained how the crucifixion was really an exultation. "He has . . . exalted them of low degree."

Questions for Discussion:

Compare the Magnificat (*Luke 1:47-55*) with the Beatitudes (*Matthew 5:3-11*). What similarities do you see? Does this suggest something about Mary having taught her Son?

Does the parable about the Rich man and Lazarus bother you? Why was the rich man condemned? Don't we all know people who cannot be helped? Why did Mary sing about the troubles of the rich?

Do the parables about pride disturb you? They should, because we know that people who don't have a healthy sense of self-worth will follow the wrong crowd and get in trouble. You may want to talk with your friends about this. Why did Mary sing about the "proud" being scattered? What sort of "pride" is involved here? Do you know people who lack a good kind of pride? Do you know people who carry around a bad kind of pride?

Only Luke tells us about these parables. Can you imagine that Mary heard them and remembered them? Can you imagine her conversations with Luke when she told him these parables?

Both Luke and Matthew tell us that John the Baptist (who was Elizabeth's son and Jesus' cousin) preached about cutting unproductive trees (*Matthew 3:7-10, Luke 3:7-9*), and Jesus didn't disagree, but Jesus said that God will give us a second chance. Ask yourself, "Is this parable about me?" If you have difficulty seeing the relation between yourself and a fruit tree, consider *Galatians 5:22-23*, "The fruit of the Spirit is love, joy, peace, patience, kindness, generosity, faithfulness, gentleness, and self-control." Are you bearing all of these kinds of fruit? Do you need a second chance?

A REFUGEE IN

ALEXANDRIA

In this session we will look at what Matthew has told us about Mary. He didn't know nearly as much as Luke, but he told us some important things. Don't go through this too quickly. It will be worth your time to have a serious discussion about the questions.

Staying Together, No Matter What.

What does it mean to be married? We are aware that weddings (the marriage ceremony) vary widely from culture to culture and time to time. Also we know that family patterns vary from place to place and time to time. In *Genesis* we see that marriages sometimes involved one husband with several wives. Today, around the world, multiple wives and husbands are uncommon. The most common "nuclear" family consists of one husband, one wife, and a child or children. In many places around the world this "nuclear" family lives in a household that includes an "extended" family that can include grandparents, uncles and aunts and their children.

Regardless of the family pattern, marriage has a central meaning and function that we find everywhere and in all eras. Marriage unites people in such a way that they are responsible for one another. Normally this means that they will live together and, if they have to move, they will move together.

If they become refugees, they will seek to stay together as refugees. That was the situation with Joseph, a builder from Nazareth, and his young wife, Mary. We'll come to their refugee experience in a little bit. First, let's take a quick look at some of Joseph's ancestors.

Women in Joseph's Heritage.

We meet Joseph and Mary in *Matthew* and *Luke. Mark* and *John* don't mention Joseph. *Matthew 1:1-16* gives us a genealogy for Joseph, beginning with Abraham, continuing through King David, and concluding with Jacob, son of Matthan, who was Joseph's father. It is a passage we often ignore, but there is at least one interesting thing about it: this list of 42 fathers and sons includes four mothers (in addition to Mary): Tamar (v. 3), Rahab (v. 5), Ruth (v. 5), and "the wife of Uriah" (v. 6). You may want to stop and read each of their stories.

Tamar lived in a time when it was shameful for a woman not to have children, and she was being prevented by her father-in-law from having children. She finally decided to take matters into her own hands (at the risk of her life) and trick her father-in-law into becoming the father of her children. Was this a sin? Read about it in *Genesis 38.* (By the way, the custom spoken of in Genesis 38:8 is behind the debate between Jesus and the Sadducees in *Matthew 22:23-33; Mark 12:18-27* and *Luke 20:27-40.*)

Rahab was quite simply a prostitute. We might imagine reasons why she had to follow this profession, but such stories will be nothing more than imagination. We don't know whether she was doing it to earn a living, whether she thought of it as service to a pagan god, or if she had some other reason. All we know is that when Joshua wanted to conquer the city of Jericho and sent spies into the city, they met Rahab and she protected them. Read her story in *Joshua 2* and *6:15-25.*

After the conquest one of the soldiers of Israel married Rahab, and she became King David's great-great grandmother (*Ruth 4:18-22*).

Ruth came from the land of Moab, and Moabites were despised. Citizens of Israel were to have nothing to do with citizens of Moab. We are told that the bad reputation of Moab went back to its founder, a man named Moab, who was the son of incest between Lot and his daughter. This was after the destruction of Sodom and Gomorrah. *Genesis* tells us that Lot and his daughters escaped and the girls thought there were no more people left on earth, so it was their duty to repopulate the world. They got their father drunk and had intercourse with him. Read about the origin of Moab in *Genesis 19:30-38.*

Much later, when the Israelites were escaping their captivity in Egypt, they passed through the land of Moab, and the kingdom of Moab became their enemy. Most of this story is told in *Numbers 21-25.* We also find in chapter 25 that the Moabites attempted to lead the Israelites away from God. It was a long time after this that Ruth became the daughter-in-law of Naomi, that they both lost their husbands, and the two women returned to Israel without any means of support.

The "wife of Uriah" has a name, Bathsheba. You can read her story in *2 Samuel 11-12.* You will find out that she and David became the parents of King Solomon.

It seems clear that Matthew thought a genealogy should be about men, but he specifically mentions these four women, and for various reasons each of them was looked down upon by others. Think about why Matthew made a point of including these four women.

King Herod Creates a Crisis.

Mary is mentioned in *Matthew 1* and *2,* but little is said about her. Furthermore, most of *Matthew's* references to her call her "mother," not "Mary." Even so, we learn that Mary had to take her baby and run away from King Herod. We can imagine what that experience was like.

Before becoming refugees, Joseph, Mary, and Jesus had apparently spent a year-and-a-half or more in Bethlehem. We know about that time period because Herod wanted to kill all boys under the age of two (*Matthew 2:16*). Not only that, but by the time the Magi came with their gifts, the family was living in a house rather than the stable where Jesus had been born (*Matthew 2:11*). Perhaps they had settled in and intended to stay in Bethlehem. Perhaps Mary had good memories of Bethlehem where she watched Jesus begin to crawl, take his first steps, say his first words.

We suspect that Mary was quite young, probably in her teens. We also suspect that Joseph was relatively old, perhaps old enough to be her father. Joseph disappears from the Gospels sometime after Jesus becomes a teen-ager, and we suspect that he died, leaving Jesus to care for the family business and for his mother.

We can look at a modern road map of Israel (see pages 48-49) and see the probable route Mary and Joseph followed, because roads usually follow the same path over time, even over thousands of years. It must have been a difficult journey. The likely route would have taken them about 70 miles to the coast where they could book passage on a ship to the city of Alexandria.

Alexandria was a "new" cosmopolitan city on the coast of Egypt. By "new," we mean that it was only about three centuries old, while most cities in the Roman Empire had existed for a thousand years or even many thousands of years. As a "new" city it wasn't ruled by a collection of "old" families. New people were relatively welcome. Furthermore, Alexandria was large. It was the second largest city in the Roman Empire, second only to Rome itself. Alexandria also had a large Jewish population, perhaps it was the largest Jewish population in the world, even larger than the population of Jerusalem. All in all, Alexandria was a good place for Joseph to take his young wife and child. Employment was available. They could join a Synagogue and make friends. Egypt was the "breadbasket" of the Roman Empire, so the cost of living was affordable.

Matthew gives us another reason for Joseph and Mary to become refugees in Alexandria. Matthew tells us that this happenstance permitted a prophecy to be fulfilled: "Out of Egypt I have called my son." (*Hosea 11:1; Matthew 2:15*.)

Questions for Discussion

Why do you think Matthew made a point of including four women when he wrote the genealogy?

Do you think that Joseph explained to Mary why they had to grab whatever they could carry and leave? Do you think that Mary understood the danger? Did this experience of running away, not really knowing where she was going, and depending entirely on her husband and on God, influence her later life? How?

If you had to flee from your home today, where would you go? Why?

Why do you think Mary and Joseph went to Egypt? (a) They had relatives there. (b) They knew people who had moved there? (c) To fulfill a prophecy? Did they consciously want to fulfill a prophecy? When we do what the Lord has ordained for us, do we sometimes do so for personal reasons? Think about your life. As you look back, you see that you have been guided by God, but did it seem so at the time?

MARY TRAVELS
AND MEETS LUKE

Here's a good question: How was Ephesus an important part of the Christmas story? The answer has to do with both Luke and Mary living there.

Ephesus: An Important City.

Let's think about Ephesus. It was a major seaport on the south-western edge of modern-day Turkey, and it was the fourth largest city in the Roman Empire. It was also firmly anchored in paganism. The Ephesian Temple of Artemis (or Diana) was unbelievably large, and was considered one of the seven wonders of the ancient world. Three-quarters of its area consisted of a forest of marble columns, more than 100 of them, many more than necessary to support the roof. The columns had been donated by King Croesus, who may have been the model for the mythical King Midas who turned everything to gold. By donating these columns, King Croesus was showing the world how wealthy he was.

These were not the columns you may have seen on government buildings in Washington, D.C. or on old downtown post offices. They were about 60 feet tall and so big around that it would take five or six adults with arms outstretched to circle one. Today the only thing left at the site of that great wonder of the ancient world is one column, constructed from mismatched pieces. If we visit the British Museum in London, we can examine the only base of any of the columns to have survived from ancient times. These are the only remains of this once great structure.

*The only surviving column base from the Temple of
Artemis (or Diana) in Ephesus. The carvings represent
Greek/Roman gods and goddesses, and are about seven
feet tall. This column base is in the British Museum,
London.*

The temple may be gone and even forgotten, but recent studies make it clear that the religion of Artemis ruled the city. There were other temples to other gods and goddesses, but in Ephesus, Artemis was the queen. The book of *Acts* represents this fact well when it tells us about the "riot of the silversmiths." (*Acts 19:21-41.*)

Indeed the cult of Artemis was very important to the local economy. There was a big "Artemis industry" that employed many people. The people of Ephesus claimed that Artemis and her brother, Apollo, had been born in a remote location about five miles from the city, and every year there was a grand procession from the great Temple to the birthplace. Tourists came from far away to participate in this great festival, as well as coming throughout the year simply to visit the Temple. Tourist money was important to the Ephesian economy.

It is interesting that the city of Ephesus had been able to convince so many people that it was the "hometown" of the goddess because another tradition told of her having been born on an island in the Aegean Sea. That story was that the twins were born as a result of the infidelity of their father, Zeus (king of the gods). Zeus' wife, Hera, was angry and threatened to punish the woman who had so attracted her husband. Hera declared that the children could not be born anywhere on earth, so Zeus provided a floating island as the birthplace. The island later anchored to the bottom of the sea. Obviously this story is incompatible with the assertion that Artemis and Apollo were born on the mainland of Asia Minor, but the people of Ephesus had good public relations skills and convinced people that their city was the best place to worship Artemis.

In spite of its paganism, the port of Ephesus was too important a trading and population center for the first Christian evangelists to ignore. Paul focused his evangelism on major population centers that were also seaports. Sailors visiting the seaports could became evangelists for the religion of Jesus. Ephesus was exactly the kind of city where Paul wanted to proclaim the Gospel. The strategic location of Ephesus was obvious to others as well. Apollos was a brilliant preacher who made a point of coming to Ephesus (*Acts 18:24,* etc.).

The Apostle John brought Mary to Ephesus.

In addition we are told by several early writers that the disciple John, son of Zebedee, ended his life in Ephesus. We are not told this in the New Testament, although the New Testament is the source of our information that John was exiled to the island of Patmos, which is not far from Ephesus (*Rev. 1:9*). The writers that tell us about John living in Ephesus are second and third generation Christians, but they have always been considered highly reliable.

In *John's Gospel* we are told that Jesus, as he hung on the cross, told John to take care of his mother, Mary (*John 19:26-27*). If John came to Ephesus, Mary came with him. Today there are two stories about where Mary ended her life: either in Jerusalem or in Ephesus. When we consider the traditions carefully it makes great sense that Mary spent her last years in "suburban" Ephesus.

Luke, the Historian, came to Ephesus.

Luke, the Gospel writer, was not one of the twelve disciples. He was a historian who wrote the New Testament books of *Luke* and *Acts* mostly based on interviews with people who had "been there." Yes, Luke knew first hand the things he had experienced while traveling with Paul, but most of what he wrote was based on interviews, and he must have been very excited to have the opportunity to interview the mother of his Lord! Luke and Paul stayed in Ephesus for about two years, and we can imagine him going to Mary's house repeatedly and asking her more questions.

We can make a good guess about his questions and her answers because there are several sections in Luke's Gospel that give us information not found in other Gospels. As we think about this "special" information, it sometimes seems that no one other than Mary would have known about it. For example, no one else was present when the Angel Gabriel came to Mary. Also, who, besides the boy's mother, would remember the time Jesus "hung out" in the Jerusalem Temple while his parents worried that he was lost forever? (*Luke 2:41-52.*)

Mary Remembers Jesus' Sermon in Nazareth.

Let's look at another example. Luke tells us that Jesus returned to Nazareth for a visit and was invited to preach in the Synagogue. (It seems that Jesus had moved to the town of Capernaum. Probably the job opportunities were better there than in his hometown.) In his sermon he spoke about the fact that God loves everyone, not just the hometown folks. (*Luke 4;16-30.*) He spoke about Elijah having been sent to minister to a woman in Sidon, north of Israel and a center of pagan worship. He spoke about Elisha (Elijah's disciple) healing Naaman the Syrian, who would normally be an enemy of Israel. Jesus' sermon really upset people, and Clarence Jordan's "Cotton Patch" version tells us, "the whole congregation blew a gasket. They jumped up, ran him out of town, and dragged him to the top of the hill on which their city was built, with the intention of pushing him off. But he got up and walked right through the middle of the whole mob and went on his way."

Who, besides Mary, could have told Luke about that incident?

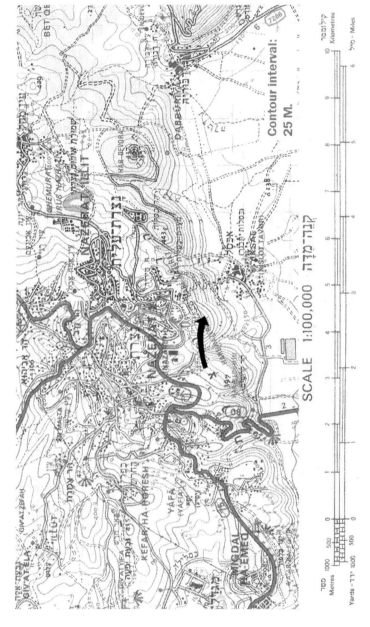

Page 40:
A topographic map showing the terrain around Nazareth.
If you are not familiar with such maps, notice the "wavy"
contour lines. They indicate elevation. If the lines are
close together, they indicate a steep hill. When they blend
together they indicate a cliff. The arrow points to a steep
hill south of the town. However there is no cliff. Source:
Israel Grid, Survey of Israel, 1992.

Let's think about this for a bit. First, Luke tells us that the crowd was so angry they tried to kill Jesus by throwing him off a cliff, but there is no cliff anywhere near Nazareth. This should indicate to us that there is something "behind" this story, if we can only imagine it.

Ask yourself what qualities God would want for the mother of God's own Son. Make a list now. What characteristics would you notice if you met Mary face-to-face and spent some time with her?

I suggest that one of the necessary qualities for the mother of God's own Son would be a healthy sense of humor. Jesus was a precocious child, and precocious children tend to get into special kinds of trouble, such as forgetting the time and hanging out in the Temple. How would you respond if you found your son after three days of searching?

When I say "sense of humor" it doesn't mean that Mary simply laughed at problems. She had to correct Jesus. Even though he was the Son of God, he had to learn things about this world as he grew up. We read in *Luke 2:48* that Mary explained very clearly to Jesus how he had done the wrong thing. Our question is what attitude she would have had when she explained things to him. Would she be boiling angry? Would she be exasperated? Or would she understand that the child means well, but needs to grow "in wisdom?" In other words, would she be able to remember the incident with a smile?

What about the Gospel writer, Luke? He sometimes seems overly serious, emphasizing the things that threaten to go bad. If there is a riot, Luke tells us about it in detail. At the end of the Book of Acts he tells us in great detail about a storm at sea, while other authors might have described it in a couple of sentences. In contrast, he tells us nothing about the church in Beroea (or Berea, *Acts 17:10-14, 20:4*), possibly because nothing exciting happened there. Luke seems to have had little sense of humor and have been very interested in near catastrophes, such as a crowd wanting to kill Jesus.

Now imagine the day when Luke sat down with Mary, took out his wax tablet and stylus (tools they used for taking notes in the ancient world), and said, "Tell me more." Mary responded by saying, "Ah yes, I must tell you about the time Jesus returned to Nazareth and preached in the synagogue." She told about the sermon, laughed, and said (jokingly), "Ah, they were so mad! They would have liked to throw him over a cliff!"

How do we conclude that Mary was Luke's source for this information? After all, we also read about Jesus returning to Nazareth in *Matthew 13:54-58* and *Mark 6:1-6*. There's a big difference. *Matthew* and *Mark* simply give us brief summaries, quite a contrast with the rich detail in Luke. Mary would have remembered the details and found the hard-headedness of the congregation members funny. For her it was a joke, but for Luke it was one of his beloved near catastrophes. He wrote on the wax tablet, "Tried to throw him off a cliff!"

Questions:

List some qualities God would require in the mother of Jesus.

What was Mary's attitude when she "corrected" the 12-year-old Jesus when she found him in the Temple?

Have you ever dealt with a child's "misbehavior" effectively because you showed your wise sense of humor?

Has a preacher's sermon ever left you feeling angry? What made you angry? If no sermon has ever made you angry, can you imagine such a sermon?

Read the stories Jesus spoke of in his sermon. The Elijah story is in *1 Kings 17*. The Elisha story is in *2 Kings 5*. Find Zarephath and Syria on a map. Can you understand why the people got angry with Jesus?

Final Note

That's some of how I see Mary's memories. Some of it is based on fact, some of it is based on conjecture, which is a fancy word for "guess," but I think the guesses are reasonable.

Never forget that there were lots more disciples than the twelve. The twelve were the "inner circle," but without other disciples to back them up nothing would have happened. Some of those disciples were women, and one of these woman disciples was Mary. As for us, we are also disciples. No one may remember us, but we are backing-up the work of God. Don't ever forget what a disciple is supposed to do: Listen for the word of God, then whenever you're sure God has spoken, say, "Yes." Then spread the word.

I hope you have found friends with whom you could share this study. I hope the process of thinking about Mary as a real person has been a blessing to you. I hope this has helped you learn something about the Bible that you didn't know, and that it has also helped you think about your own life. The Bible reflects each of our lives.

ADDITIONAL RESOURCES

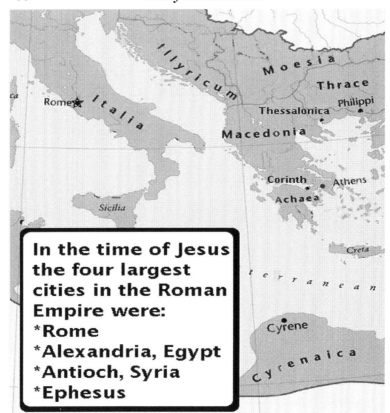

In the time of Jesus the four largest cities in the Roman Empire were:
*Rome
*Alexandria, Egypt
*Antioch, Syria
*Ephesus

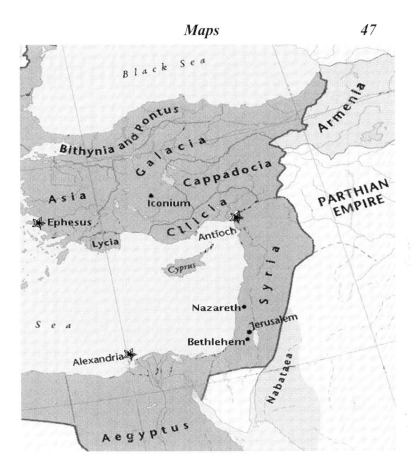

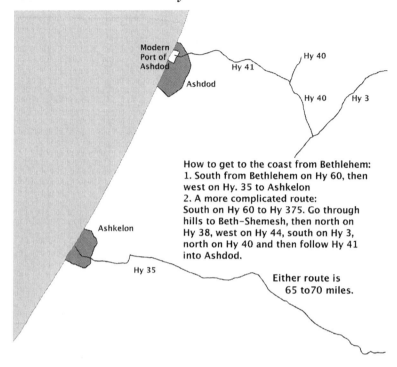

How to get to the coast from Bethlehem:
1. South from Bethlehem on Hy 60, then west on Hy. 35 to Ashkelon
2. A more complicated route:
South on Hy 60 to Hy 375. Go through hills to Beth-Shemesh, then north on Hy 38, west on Hy 44, south on Hy 3, north on Hy 40 and then follow Hy 41 into Ashdod.

Either route is 65 to70 miles.

How did Joseph, Mary and Jesus get to Egypt?

They could have traveled by land on the "wilderness road" (Acts 8:26), but this would have been very difficult. By this time Jesus might have been an 18 month old toddler, more difficult to travel with than a babe in arms.

More likely, they went to the coast and found passage on a ship bound for Alexandria. Alexandria was the second largest city in the Roman Empire and had a large Jewish population. The family would have found friends there and Joseph would have found employment.

They didn't want to go north to Jerusalem, even though they could get on a main road to the coast from the capitol city.

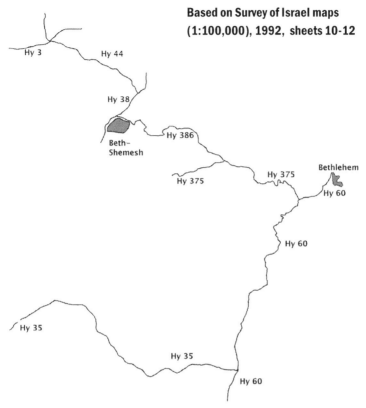

**Based on Survey of Israel maps
(1:100,000), 1992, sheets 10-12**

In hilly or mountainous areas, modern roads and ancient roads tend to follow the same paths. Thus we can look at modern roads in Israel and suggest a couple of routes between Bethlehem and the coast.

One route is simple: Hy 60 south to Hy 35, then take a right turn and travel west to Ashkelon (a city where Herod the Great had built major structures). But Roman soldiers might have been on this road.

More likely the family turned off on Hy 375, going into the hill country toward Beth Shemesh, then on to Ashdod (which the Romans called Azotus - Acts 8:40).

HOW OLD WAS MARY WHEN SHE WAS IN EPHESUS?

Perhaps Mary was no longer alive when John came to Ephesus. This is a matter worth thinking about.

First there is the problem of life-span in the ancient world. Often people died in their 30s because of infection, disease, murder or disaster. However, if a person remained healthy and out of trouble, an ancient person might live as long as many people live in our time.

Second, Jesus was probably born in 5 BC. (When our calendar was established, someone calculated incorrectly. Year zero was not actually Jesus' birth year.)

Third, Mary was probably very young when Jesus was born.

Fourth, Paul and Luke were in Ephesus in 54 AD.

These four facts combined with any reasonable assumptions lead us to conclude that Mary was in her 70s when Paul and Luke were in Ephesus.

For example, if Mary was 14 when Jesus was born, she would have been 73 in the year 54 AD. If she was 16 when Jesus was born, she would have been 75.

Today we all know people who are healthy, alert and active at age 75. It is not strange to think that Mary could have met Luke in Ephesus.

SOME OTHER THINGS
MARY REMEMBERED

How do we know what Mary thought and remembered? We don't have anything that she wrote. We don't have any of those bits of evidence that lead us to think that we understand what another person thinks. So we can only guess about her thoughts. However, there are some clues that help us make some guesses that are not just wild fantasies. As I have said, I think we can find some of her memories in the Gospels, and I think we have good reasons for thinking we can find her memories.

Mary Lived in Ephesus

In the final session we said that John took his new "mother," Mary, to Ephesus. How do we know this? A second-generation leader of the church (named Polycarp) tells us that John became a resident of Ephesus. Then a third generation Christian (named Tertullian) tells us that John, as the leader of the Christians in Ephesus, sent Polycarp to the neighboring city of Smyrna to be their bishop. We are not told that John brought Mary with him, but certainly he would have. Thus Luke would have met her there.

The city lay in a valley, and the residential areas were on the hillsides next to the valley. If you visit Ephesus and go south (which is seriously up-hill), when you get near the top of the hill you will find a stone house which is visited by thousands of pilgrims each year. It is said to be the house where Mary lived her last years, and although this particular building is probably not the one Mary lived in, I see no good reason to doubt that she lived on this site, or at least nearby.

Mary Remembered that Women were Important in Jesus' Ministry

Unlike some early Christians, Luke understood that women are included in God's plan for this world and the world to come, and I think Mary's memories of her son's ministry helped Luke understand this. Of the four Gospel-writers, Luke is the only one who recognizes that Jesus could not have spent time traveling with and teaching the twelve disciples if it hadn't been for the support of women. Here's how Luke writes about it: "He went on . . . proclaiming and bringing the Good News of the Kingdom of God. The twelve were with him, as well as some women who had been cured of evil spirits and infirmities: Mary, called Magdalene, from whom seven demons had gone out, and Joanna, the wife of Herod's steward Chuza, and Susanna, and many others, who pro-vided for them out of their resources." (*Luke 8:1-3.*) *Matthew* and *Mark* also tell us that women who observed his death on the cross had been "ministering" to him (*Matt. 27:55-56; Mark 15:40-41*), but Luke is much more explicit about monetary support.

Why is this information only in *Luke's Gospel*? Doesn't it sound like the sort of thing a mother, who is naturally concerned about her son's career, would know? Some reading this book, both men and women, will be old enough to have adult children. Do you worry about these adults? Do you wonder how they're getting along? Can you confirm the likelihood that Mary would have made a point of knowing and remembering where the money came from to support her son's ministry?

I think Mary not only told Luke. I think it quite possible that Mary was one of the "many others." You may ask, "If Mary was involved, why didn't Luke mention it?" Maybe Mary didn't want to "toot her own horn" when Luke was interviewing her so her name didn't get attached to this group of women, but she knew about them, and that's why Luke was able to tell us about them.

Everyone is Important, Even Samaritans

One time Jesus was asked about being a neighbor, and Jesus told a story about a man who was accosted by robbers as he traveled from Jerusalem to Jericho (a steep descent with plenty of potential ambush sites). A couple of "good" people passed by "on the other side," probably avoiding the man because they thought he was dead. Then a Samaritan (not a "good" person) stopped, rendered first aid, took him to an inn where he could receive care, and guaranteed financial payment for the care. (*Luke 10:29-37.*) Surely Mary had heard this story, and surely she understood that this Samaritan was one of Jesus' true brothers. The fact that this parable appears only in Luke suggests the possibility that Mary told Luke about it.

Perhaps Mary was with Jesus when a group of ten lepers called from a nearby hill, "Have mercy on us!" (*Luke 17:11-19.*) Obviously they knew who Jesus was. They knew his reputation for healing (see *Luke 5:12-15*). Jesus did not disappoint them. He sent them to the priest, as required in *Leviticus 14*. No doubt they were all consumed both with joy and with concern for the multi-day purification ritual they would have to undergo, so it's not surprising that they didn't stop to say, "Thank you" . . . except that one of the ten did stop. He was a Samaritan.

Why is Luke the only gospel writer to tell us these good things about Samaritans? We can imagine that Mary remembered them and told Luke about God's love for Samaritans. John also tells us something important about Jesus and Samaritans. One time when Jesus was passing through the region of Samaria, he saw a woman drawing water from the town well. He asked her for a drink, and this led to a profound discussion about God's love for all people. (*John 4:4-42.*) As John tells it, it is a long story. Clearly John understood the significance of Jesus' acceptance of the "not-good" Samaritans. Maybe John and Mary, who had both seen Jesus at work, discussed the matter.

Remembering a Wedding

John tells us a story that no other Gospel writer mentions. John may not have had to hear about this incident from Mary, because he may have been there and seen what happened and remembered it. Maybe he talked about it with Mary in later years, or maybe not. Regardless, the story of the wedding certainly tells us something about Mary.

The family went to a wedding in the town of Cana. At the wedding feast the guests drank all of the wine. With no more wine the party was doomed to failure, but Mary prevailed on her son to fix the problem, so he did. Read about it in *John 2:1-10*. John calls it the first sign that Jesus was the Messiah.

For our purposes we need to think about the conversation between Jesus and his mother. It is an indirect conversation (maybe like a conversation you have had with one of your children). Mary says, "They have no wine," making an implicit request. Jesus makes an oblique response, "My time has not come." Mary ignores what Jesus said, and speaks to the wine steward, "Do whatever he tells you." Then Jesus performs the miracle.

We can see that when John wrote about this incident he was making a comment about the wonderful respect Jesus had for his mother. You may object and say that this incident shows the opposite, because Jesus rejected his mother's request. There are at least two things to say in response.

The first thing to say is "common sense." In spite of what Jesus said, he immediately acted to fulfill his mother's request: "Fill up the jars with water." It seems likely that this wedding involved good friends of the family, and neither Mary nor Jesus wanted their good friends to be embarrassed. This fits with Jesus' consistent compassion, and compassion was no doubt one of Mary's core qualities as well.

The second thing to say has to do with biblical scholarship. Greek grammar occasionally differs from English grammar, and this can lead scholars to disagree with one another about the best translation of some phrases. In this account did Jesus intend to say, "My time has not yet come," or did Jesus intend to say something else? Some scholars have argued that Jesus intended to say, "Has not my time come?" In other words, Jesus may have actually been announcing the formal beginning of his ministry. Which translation is most accurate is a highly technical matter, and scholars debate it, but John does go on to tell us that the wedding miracle was Jesus' "first sign." In fact, his "time" had come, and Mary knew it.

Remembering a Joyous Funeral

Let's turn to another item that appears only in *Luke's Gospel* (*Luke 7:11-17*). Jesus and his disciples go to a town called Nain and find a funeral procession coming out through the gate in the town wall. Pay close attention.

Maybe Nain was the smallest city you could have that would have a wall. As a small city, it probably didn't have many gates, because every gate in your wall required that someone guard it, and Nain could only afford so many guards. Also, the gates were probably not really large. A large city would have gates big enough to have a two-lane road going through them. But the larger the gate, the bigger and more expensive the doors to the gate, and the more guards you would need. Nain probably had one-lane gates.

Jesus always traveled with a crowd. We think about him traveling with the 12 disciples, but we know that there were others who traveled regularly with him, and there were still others who came out to hear him whenever they could. When he came to the city of Nain, he was with a pretty big group of people, and to get into the city, they would have had to go through the gate two, or at most three at a time.

Right then there was a funeral for a young man who had left his widowed mother alone. The grief was fresh for everyone and he had been her only support. Everyone felt the mother's grief and distress.

There was a requirement that people were to be buried the same day that they died, and the cemeteries were always outside of town. All of these people were coming with the body through the gate as they went to the cemetery outside the walls.

Two groups of people were trying to go through a small gate in opposite directions at the same time. As they approached the gate, neither group knew the other group was coming at them. It was chaos.

Hold that picture in your mind for a bit while we think about something that Jesus had learned from Joseph. Joseph was a contractor, a builder. Jesus had learned from Joseph that to get things done you had to get your hands dirty. This is important.

Two people stood clear of the crowds. One was Jesus. He stood back assessing the situation. The other was Mary. She stood back observing her son.

It didn't take long for Jesus to figure out what was going on. He understood that the widow no longer had any source of support in this world. He decided quickly what he needed to do. He got his hands dirty.

If you flip back to the laws of Moses in the first five books of the Bible, you find that any association with a dead body made a person ritually unclean. Such a person would have to go through purification rituals. In that society, no one would associate with an undertaker. They didn't want death to touch them. Purification was sometimes a complicated process. (See the procedure described in *Numbers 19:11-13*. See also *Numbers 5:2*. There was also a special regulation related to priests, *Leviticus 21:11*, which is important for understanding the Parable of the Good Samaritan, *Luke 10:25-37*. The priest who passed the injured man "on the other side" was afraid the man might be dead.)

Jesus didn't hesitate. He marched into the crowd, up to the people who were carrying the body. The body certainly wasn't in a casket. It might have been in a basket, or it might even have just been covered by a shroud. Jesus laid his hands on the basket, or even on the body. Either contact was enough to make him unclean and make people want to avoid him.

Jesus told the young man to get up, and presented him, alive, to his mother.

He *could* do it because he was the Son of God. He was *willing* to do it because he had learned from his earthly father, Joseph. Joseph had taught Jesus that honest work does not defile a person.

Luke is the only author who tells us about this funeral at Nain. How could he have known about it? Who did he ever talk with who had seen this miracle? Of course, Mary, the mother of Jesus, was there.

Some other Questions about Death and Life.

We might ask why Jesus didn't raise everyone from the dead. We might ask why Jesus didn't simply destroy death. Answer: That's not what he came for. Life on this earth is not our ultimate goal. We need to move aside for new generations. Our goal is beyond this earth.

In the first century there were many magicians in the Roman Empire. We see a hint of how widespread these people were in *Acts 19:11-20*. Some of these magicians specialized in raising the dead. (Of course the circumstances had to be right for them to perform this magic trick. Of course the circumstances were never "right" whenever you and they were together. That wasn't their fault. They would still tell you, with a straight face, that they had the gift of raising the dead. They had done it when you weren't present.)

Jesus was different from these so-called magicians. Jesus never claimed to be a magician, and Jesus never claimed to specialize in raising the dead. As a matter of fact, he only raised three people, and each time it was without fanfare.

When he raised the young daughter of Jairus, he sent almost everyone out of the room. When she got up from her deathbed he simply gave some very practical advice: "Give her something to eat." This story is in both *Mark (5:21-43)* and *Luke (8:40-56)*, and both Gospels are very clear that Jesus didn't want any publicity about the fact that he raised the girl.

When he raised his good friend, Lazarus (*John 11:1-44*) he was also matter-of-fact, as he had been with the little girl. He said, "Unbind him and let him go." Once again there was no attempt to gain publicity, although *John 11:45-53* suggests that raising Lazarus led to official opposition. The officials were afraid that Jesus would seek publicity and use his notoriety in an attempt to lead a political revolt against the Roman Empire. The Gospels make it clear that Jesus never wanted to lead a political revolution.

When Jesus visited Nain he was, as usual, matter-of-fact. Miracles are not for show. Miracles are for the purpose of serving people. You may want to compare Jesus with Elijah. The prophet Elijah raised a young boy (*2 Kings 17:19-24.*) Ask yourself how Jesus and Elijah are similar and how they are different at this point.

We can imagine that the miracle at Nain happened so effortlessly that many who would have witnessed it were unaware. Others forgot because it was not spectacular. By this time Jesus' mother was (at least sometimes) traveling with him, and she remembered. As we have said, Mary must have been compassionate, and she would especially remember her Son's works of compassion.

Mothers take pride in many different qualities and accomplishments of their children. Some mothers focus on sports ability. Some mothers focus on talent in music or art. Some mothers focus on business success. Mary focused on compassion.

Did Jesus Reject his Family?

Jesus claimed as family members everyone who does the will of God (*Luke 8:21*) But in *Luke 11:27,* we are told that one time when Jesus was teaching, someone in the crowd shouted out, "Blessed is the womb that bore you and the breasts that nursed you!" This was probably a common expression in those days, a way of praising someone by praising their mother. (We will not likely find this in other literary sources, because it is a folk expression, out of the view of the literary elite.) Probably Jesus heard it a lot, and he turned it into an occasion for teaching. His usual response would be, "Blessed, rather, are those who hear the word of God and obey it!" (*Luke 11:28*, which is about the same thing as *Luke 8:21*.)

This is difficult, because it sounds as if it is a rejection of his mother. Jesus' point was, "I'm telling you some important stuff, and you are trying to get out of having to hear how serious it is by praising my mother. You think that I can get distracted, and that I certainly wouldn't say anything that makes someone think I don't like my mother. You're wrong. I will do anything to keep on track and make you understand what I'm saying." This same issue came up in Matthew and *Mark*, as well as in *Luke* (*Matt. 12:46-50, Mark 3:31-35*). Jesus would not be distracted by people saying things like, "Oh, your mother must be proud of you."

Mary was not upset by this. She was even willing to talk with Luke about it.

Imagine Luke visiting Mary in her house on the hill. He says, "I've heard that sometimes Jesus said that you weren't all that important," and Mary said, "Of course I'm not. The only thing that's important is God's work in this world."

Now Mary must have been a forceful woman, but she was also humble, and she would have told Luke about having heard people cry out blessings on her as the mother, with Jesus keeping them on track by saying, "Blessed are the ones who do what God wants." She also would have told Luke that Jesus took the Ten   Commandments seriously, and reserved some of his strongest condemnations for people who purposely   misinterpreted the law so that they could avoid taking care of their father and mother. (It is *Mark* who especially tells us about this teaching, *7:9-12.)*

If You Need More Questions for Discussion

Think about the three qualities shared by all disciples. Do you agree that Mary was a disciple?

Are you a disciple? (This may be a difficult question. You don't have to answer it if you don't want to, but you should think about it.) Why or why not?

John tells us about the attitude that many people had about Samaritans. For these people, the word "Samaritan," was essentially a curse word. (*John 8:48*.) Why was Jesus' attitude so different?

Are there groups of people your friends don't "like?" How might you tell them kindly about Jesus' attitude toward those whom many don't like?

The widow of Zarephath lived in the territory where everyone worshipped the pagan god Baal. (See *1 Kings 17:9.* The city/kingdom of Sidon was north of Israel and was an important seaport in the days of Elijah. You may want to take some time to discuss the whole account of Elijah and the widow.) Naaman the Syrian asked permission to accompany his king when the king worshipped the pagan god, Rimmon. (*See 2 Kings 5:18-19*). Why do you think God (the real God) loves these worshippers of idols? Does that make idol-worship all right? Can a person who worships an idol be part of Jesus' family?

You may also want to discuss Elisha's servant, Ghazi, *2 Kings 5:19-27.*

*When Mary was a new mother, a righteous,
elderly man, Simeon, prophesied to Mary: ". . . a
sword will pierce your own soul . . ." (Luke 2:35).
Luke is the only Gospel writer to tell us about this.
The statue pictured here is in the Frauenkierche,
Munich, Germany.*

AN IMAGINED INTERVIEW
BETWEEN LUKE AND MARY

There are old monasteries all over the eastern
Mediterranean, and each has a library. In these libraries are
uncatalogued ancient manuscripts. It is difficult to get
permission to visit these archives, but a scholar who can get
permission just might turn up something really interesting.
Maybe they could find the transcript of an interview that
Luke had with the mother of Jesus. I dreamed about visiting
such an ancient archive, and here is what I discovered in my
dream:

Luke: What was Pilate like?

Mary: Ach! He was no good! You know, he was the guy
who commanded the soldiers, and all he cared about was
soldiers. Soldiers and himself. He didn't care about the
people.

You know, he said we needed an aqueduct . . . but
we had gotten along for a thousand years or more without an
aqueduct! He wanted to build it for his own glory. I think he
was competing with King Herod to see who could build the
most monuments.

So he robbed the Temple treasury. Ach! He asked
permission, but he had the army! The people didn't like it,
and they protested, but he sent in his army with clubs, and
killed a bunch of them.

Luke: Was Jesus involved in that protest?

Mary: No. No. He was up in Galilee then. But he heard about it, and was upset, just like all of us were.
I know he thought a lot about it, because later, when he was teaching the people, he talked about it.

You know about the tower that fell down? No? Well one of the big land owners wanted to build a big tower next to his vineyard so that his guards could keep watch and keep thieves out. But he didn't hire a very good architect. He should have hired my husband, Joseph. He would have built a really good tower. Ah, me, but my husband, peace be with him, was no longer with us.

Anyway the tower wasn't well designed, and the boss didn't know what he was doing, and the whole thing fell down while they were building it, and killed seven good workers. Yes, it was too bad.

Well, you know that whenever bad things happen to anybody there are always people who want to say that if they were better people the bad things wouldn't happen. Those are the kind of people who said that the men killed by Pilate's army guys were at fault. They say that they must have been some kind of secret sinners. They say they should have just stayed home and kept quiet. Those same kind of people said that the men killed by the tower collapse must have done something to make God angry with them.

Jesus said they are wrong. God didn't cause Pilate to kill those men, and God didn't cause the tower to collapse, but he said that each of us needs to keep our hands clean, because we might die any time. Those people who were killed weren't any worse than any of us. I remember exactly what he said. He said, "Unless you repent, you will perish just as they did."

Luke: That sounds like he was saying that most of us are going to die horrible deaths, and be taken by Satan.

Mary: Ach, no! That's not what he meant. He just meant that we need to be more thoughtful about how we follow God. We need to repent. We need to turn around from

how we are living and live with God every day.
Haven't you heard what he said about the fig tree?

Luke: He condemned one that didn't bear fruit.

Mary: No, no, no! That was about a tree that he had
passed many times in his travels, and he knew that it was
a useless tree. But he didn't give up on anyone or
anything very easily. Many times I heard him tell a
parable about a fig tree. He said that there was a farmer
who was upset that his fig tree wasn't bearing. He said it
hadn't had any fruit for three years, and ordered it cut
down. But the manager of the farm convinced him to give
the tree another chance. The manager said, "Let me dig
around it and throw in some good manure. We'll see if
good care doesn't help it. Next year, if it bears fruit, then
you know you have a good tree, but if then it doesn't
bear, you can cut it down."
   You know what Jesus meant when he told that
parable, don't you? He meant that we're like fig trees.
God is like the manager. God doesn't give up easily on
people, because God loves each of us.
   So when Jesus said that we need to repent, he
wasn't saying that God hates us. He was saying that God
loves the people killed by Pilate's soldiers, and God loves
the tower builders, and God loves each of us, but we have
the freedom to go away from God. We need to turn
around. We need to repent. And God gives us the
opportunity to repent.

Luke: You make it sound so simple. God loves us. I
believe that, or at least I'm struggling to believe it. I know
that the other gods, Zeus and all of those gods, really hate
us, and Jesus showed us a God that doesn't hate us . . .
but don't we have to pay for our sins? I look around and I
see people who are paying for their sins. There are so
many people who are sick and crippled and in trouble.
Haven't they sinned?

Mary: Ach! Don't you know *Job*? God doesn't want people to be sick or crippled. God wants people to be good and have a good life.

You should know that Jesus healed a lot of people. If you don't know that, you need to find it out.

I remember this one woman . . . she was bent over at the waist . . . like this. She couldn't straighten up. She always had to look at the ground. She was a good woman . . . as good as you or me. One Sabbath she came to the synagogue, and Jesus was there. Right then he stopped his teaching and said, "Woman, you are set free!" and you know what? She straightened up. Looked like everyone else. And she shouted praise to God.

But, oh, my, the leaders of the synagogue got mad at Jesus that day. They said he had done work on the Sabbath by causing her to be healed. They said he could have gone and healed her any other day of the week. Why do it on the Sabbath?

Jesus wouldn't hear it. First he told them that they are allowed to take their animals to water on the Sabbath. That means they have to loosen their halter. This woman was in a sort-of halter. Shouldn't she be let free?

Then he said that Satan causes this kind of ailment, because Satan wants bad things for us. But God is against Satan. God wants good things for us. So, Jesus said that the Sabbath is the best time to heal someone, because when they are healed, they are set free from Satan.

That's why we need to be right with God. Because God wants good things for us.

———————————————————

The manuscript breaks off there. We don't know what else they talked about, but it is clear that Luke learned a lot from the mother of Jesus. He learned more than what Jesus did and said. He found out that she was a real student of her son's teaching, and she could explain it.

She knew that Jesus expected everyone to have a place in God's kingdom. A couple of weeks ago we saw how she understood that men and women are equal in God's sight. Also those who are sick or crippled are equal to anyone else. Gentiles are just as good as Jews. It is a radical thing to realize how much God loves everyone, and Mary was a radical.

NOTES

Pages 15-16: Sherman, Henry A. and Charles Foster Kent. *The Children's Bible*. NY: Scribner's, 1922, p. 281.

Pages 18-19: Brown, Raymond E. *An Introduction to the New Testament (The Anchor Bible Reference Library)*. NY: Doubleday, 1997, pp. 229-232. Brown also sets these criteria forth in a number of other books and articles.

Pages 35-37: Recent scholarly books on the background to the religion of Artemis in Ephesus include: Immendörfer, Michael. *Ephesians and Artemis*, 2017, and Rogers, Guy Maclean. *The Mysteries of Artemis of Ephesos*. Yale U.P., 2012.

Page 38: An interesting book that presents the arguments for Mary having lived in Ephesus is Deutsch, Bernard F. *Our Lady of Ephesus*. Milwaukee: Bruce Publishing, 1965.

Page 39: Jordan, Clarence. *The Cotton Patch Version of Luke and Acts: Jesus' Doings and Happenings*. NY: Association Press, 1969, p. 25.

Page 55, on the translation of John 2:4, see A. Vanhoye, "Interrogation johannique et exegese de Cana (Jn 2,4)," *Biblica* 55 (1974) 157-67 (159-62), cited by Bearsley, Patrick J., "Mary, the Perfect Disciple: A   Paradigm for Mariology," *Theological Studies,* v. 41, #3, 1980, 461-504 (p. 485).

Page 64: The tower collapse. See Luke 13:4. This local disaster is reported only by Luke.

Made in the USA
Middletown, DE
30 November 2019